The
LITTLE
BOOK *of*
QUITTING

Sterling Publishing Co., Inc.
New York

Published by Sterling Publishing Co., Inc.
387 Park Avenue South, New York, NY 10016

ISBN 1-4027-3132-9

Library of Congress Cataloging-in-Publication Data
available upon request

7 9

Manufactured in Canada

IMPORTANT WARNING!

Unless you have already quit, do not attempt to do so, or even to cut down, before you have read and understood the whole book.

Introduction by the Author

Imagine a drug that causes the premature death of one in every two users, costs the average addict $100,000 in a lifetime, makes you feel insecure, bored, and tense, tastes foul, ruins your confidence, impedes your concentration, and has no advantages whatsoever.

Can you believe that at one time over 90% of the adult population of Western society was addicted to this drug?

Can you imagine yourself becoming addicted to such a drug? If you are a smoker, casual or otherwise, you already are an addict. The drug is nicotine.

Suppose I, being a former chain-smoker for thirty-three years, could convince you that the facts about smoking are exactly as I have described above and, furthermore, that any smoker can find it easy to quit

IMMEDIATELY AND PERMANENTLY
WITHOUT USING WILLPOWER,
GIMMICKS, OR SUBSTITUTES, AND
WITHOUT PUTTING ON WEIGHT.

What if I could further convince you that you won't miss smoking, that you'll enjoy social occasions more, and be better able to cope with stressful situations? Would you quit? Then read on. I have nothing but good news for you.

WHEN DID YOU DECIDE TO BE A SMOKER?

No. I don't mean what was the occasion of your first cigarette, but when did you decide to smoke every day?

Or did you just drift into it like every other smoker on the planet?

WILL YOU ALWAYS BE A SMOKER?

So when will you quit?

>After you've spent the $100,000?
>
>When you've crippled your health?
>
>When the time is right?

How many years have you smoked?

Do you ever wonder why it never seems like the right time to quit?

WHY DO YOU SMOKE?

Because it tastes good?

Do you eat it?

For something to do with your hands?

Try a ballpoint pen.

For oral satisfaction?

Use a pacifier.

To relieve boredom and stress, and aid relaxation and concentration?

Surely, boredom and concentration are opposites.

So are stress and relaxation.

WHAT ARE YOUR FAVORITE CIGARETTES?

First one in the morning? *Isn't that the one that tastes the worst?*

After a meal or with a drink, when answering the phone or during stress? *How can the identical cigarette out of the same pack taste different than, or have the complete opposite effect from, the one smoked an hour earlier?*

DO YOU WISH YOUR CHILDREN SMOKED?

If the answer is no, it means that you wish you were a non-smoker! So why aren't you? *Because smoking is a habit and habits are difficult to break?*

Are they? In England people are in the habit of driving on the left. If they drive in the United States, they break the habit immediately, without difficulty.

So Why Do Smokers Continue to Smoke?

For one reason and one reason only—they have fallen into the most subtle, ingenious trap that man and nature have combined to lay:

THEY ARE ADDICTED TO NICOTINE!

THE MOST POWERFUL DRUG IN THE WORLD!

Nicotine is the most powerful addictive drug known to mankind. Just one cigarette can hook you, particularly if you have been addicted previously.

A POWERFUL POISON!

The nicotine content of just one cigarette injected directly into a vein would kill you. Please don't try it. This is why those first cigarettes make you feel dizzy and sick.

THE NATURE OF THE TRAP

When the nicotine from the first cigarette leaves your body, it creates a feeling of emptiness and insecurity—the feeling that smokers know as "needing a cigarette" or "something to do with their hands."

TIGHT SHOES!

When you light the next cigarette, the nicotine is replaced, and the empty, insecure feeling immediately disappears. This is the feeling that smokers describe as a satisfaction or pleasure.

It's like wearing tight shoes just to get the pleasure of removing them!

THE LIFETIME'S CHAIN

When you extinguish the next cigarette, the nicotine leaves and the empty, insecure feeling returns. Now you need another cigarette, and another, ad infinitum, until death do you part!

THE LITTLE MONSTER

Think of that empty feeling as a tapeworm inside your body that feeds on nicotine. The true reason that any smoker continues to smoke is to feed that little nicotine monster.

YOU ARE ABOUT TO STARVE IT TO DEATH!

WHY ISN'T IT OBVIOUS?

Because it works back to front. It's when you aren't smoking that you suffer the craving. The moment you light up, it's relieved. Your brain is fooled into believing you receive a genuine pleasure or crutch.

What you are really enjoying is getting back to the state you had permanently before you lit the first cigarette.

In fact, you are simply trying to feel as relaxed as a non-smoker!

YOU NEVER GET THERE

Unless you quit. When you learn to smoke, you are merely teaching your body to become immune to a powerful poison. After a short period you only partially relieve the empty feeling. This is why the tendency is to smoke more and more.

DRUG ADDICTION OR GENUINE PLEASURE?

Genuine pleasures, like a nice vacation, create no feeling of guilt. We are pleased to boast about them and, while we would like to enjoy the pleasure more often, we do not feel deprived or miserable when not partaking of the pleasure; whereas all smokers brag how little they smoke, and even the thought of being without cigarettes creates panic.

PICTURE A HEROIN ADDICT

That terrible panic when he has no heroin and the wonderful feeling of "pleasure" when he plunges that hypodermic into a vein. Non-heroin addicts don't suffer that panicked feeling. Heroin doesn't relieve it. IT CAUSES IT! Non-smokers don't suffer the panic feeling of needing a cigarette. Neither did you before you became addicted to nicotine.

THE INCREDIBLE IRONY OF IT ALL

The only reason you or any other smoker needs or wants a cigarette is to try to get rid of your nicotine withdrawal. But it is only smokers who suffer nicotine withdrawal. Non-smokers do not. So all you are trying to do whenever you light a cigarette is feel like a non-smoker!

CHECK IT OUT

Light up now. Take six deep drags and ask yourself what it is that you are actually enjoying.

Isn't it true that it's not so much that you enjoy inhaling toxic fumes into your lungs as that you can't enjoy social occasions or cope with stress without them?

BUT DRUGS ARE DIFFICULT TO KICK

Only if you believe you get some genuine pleasure or benefit from them. Once you realize that not only does smoking destroy your health and wealth but that it actually destroys your nerves and confidence, you—or any smoker—can genuinely enjoy the process of quitting

IMMEDIATELY AND PERMANENTLY!

WHAT ABOUT THE WITHDRAWAL PANGS?

Although nicotine is the world's most powerful drug in the speed with which it hooks smokers, you are never badly hooked.

The actual physical withdrawal from nicotine is so slight that smokers only know the feeling as

I WANT A CIGARETTE!

IDENTICAL TO FOOD

Nicotine withdrawal is identical to the hunger for food. In both cases you feel irritable and empty when unable to relieve the craving, and feel confident, content, and relaxed once you satisfy the hunger or craving.

THE COMPLETE OPPOSITE
OF HUNGER

Good food genuinely tastes good, tobacco tastes foul. Food is survival, tobacco is death. Food genuinely satisfies hunger, tobacco creates the craving. Eating is a genuine pleasure we can enjoy throughout our lives. Smoking is an illusion of pleasure, an ingenious confidence trick that enslaves us for life.

I Enjoy the Taste

Most smokers can remember how foul those first cigarettes tasted, and how hard they had to work to inhale. Ask a smoker: "If you can't get your own brand, do you abstain?" A smoker would rather smoke old rope! It's like working on a pig farm. After a while you become immune to the smell. Smokers become immune to the smell of stale tobacco.

INTRODUCING
THE BIG MONSTER

From birth we are subjected to a massive, daily bombardment telling us that cigarettes relieve boredom and stress, and aid concentration and relaxation. In movies, when someone is about to be executed, his last request is always a cancer stick. In TV dramas, a husband chain-smokes outside the maternity ward. When the baby is born, cigars are handed around in celebration.

THE BRAINWASHING

This is the "Big Monster" in the mind and the real reason we find it difficult to quit. It doesn't affect us before we become hooked, because the beautiful truth is that our lives were complete before we tried those first experimental cigarettes.

But once we do, the "Little Monster" confirms the brainwashing or, more accurately, fools our brains into believing it.

THE VOID

Our children all seem to be searching for some magical elixir or prop, as if the incredible intelligence that created us (be it God or three million years of natural selection) has omitted some vital ingredient essential to our enjoyment of life or to our ability to survive.

THE INCREDIBLE MACHINE

The human body is the most sophisticated survival machine on the planet. It is complete. But children and teenagers have yet to mature. They feel insecure and vulnerable. Little wonder they turn to illusory props that guarantee they will never mature, unless and until they are free from both monsters.

LIKE CLAUSTROPHOBIA

Try forcing a claustrophobic into a confined space and he will panic. He won't suffocate, but if he believes he will, it amounts to the same thing. If you believe that you can't enjoy life or handle stress without a cigarette, you will feel miserable and insecure without one.

THE ITCH

Think of the "Little Monster" as an almost imperceptible itch that you can partially and temporarily relieve by lighting up. Like tight shoes, the longer you suffer, the greater the relief. This is why the so-called "special" cigarettes follow a period of abstinence: after a meal, exercise, sex, or whatever.

The First of the Day

The one that makes us cough our lungs up, but ironically a favorite for many smokers. That's because we've gone eight hours without nicotine. When we awake, we relieve a series of aggravations: our bladders, our thirst, etc. A non-smoker will relieve his hunger. A smoker is more likely to light a cigarette.

FOOD OR NICOTINE

Although the empty feelings are indistinguishable, nicotine will not relieve the hunger for food or vice versa. This is why I became a chain-smoker. After that first cigarette of the day, I still had the empty feeling, which was hunger for food. But to my confused brain it meant: I need another cigarette and another.

THE TUG-OF-WAR

All smokers suffer from a permanent tug-of-war:

On the one side —
It's filthy and disgusting slavery, destroying my health and wealth.

On the other side —
It's my friend, my pleasure, my crutch.

THE REALITY

It's a tug-of-war of fear. There is no genuine pleasure or crutch. The other side is also fear. The reality is: *How can I enjoy life or cope with life without cigarettes?* Both sets of fear are caused by nicotine. Non-smokers don't suffer from either.

NEITHER WILL YOU,
ONCE YOU ARE FREE!

I Wish I Were a Happy Casual Smoker

There is no such thing. With a permanent itch, the natural tendency is to scratch it continously. The natural tendency for a smoker is to become a chain-smoker. So why aren't all smokers chain-smokers? Because the effect on our health, wealth, and self-respect makes us try to control our intake of poison.

SMOKE LESS–HOOKED MORE!

The less you smoke, the less it affects your health and wealth, and the less your desire to quit. The longer you go before scratching the itch, the greater the illusion of crutch or pleasure, and the greater your desire to continue smoking.

I Can Go a Week
Without Smoking

If there is genuine pleasure, why would you want to? If there is none, why smoke at all?

I can go a week without carrots, but feel no need to boast about it. Perhaps I would boast if I'd had to discipline myself and deprive myself for a whole week. If we are proud of how little we smoke, just think how great it will feel to be free!

ALL SMOKERS LIE
TO THEMSELVES

Why? Because we sense that we've fallen into a trap and feel stupid and weak-willed because we've failed to escape from it. So we give phony reasons to justify our stupidity in order to retain some semblance of self-respect. No way do we deceive non-smokers. We don't even deceive ourselves.

I Only Enjoy Two a Day

So why do you smoke the others?

In fact, you never enjoy any.

This is why the vast majority of cigarettes are smoked subconsciously. If every time you lit a cigarette you had to be aware of that $100,000, the filth in your lungs, and that this might just be the one to trigger lung cancer, even the illusion of enjoyment would go.

WHY SMOKERS FIND IT HARD TO QUIT

Because the two monsters have fooled them into believing that they are making a genuine sacrifice, that a meal will never be as enjoyable, that they won't be able to handle stress, that they have to go through a transitional period of misery, and that, even if they succeed, they will have to resist temptation for the rest of their lives.

THE ADDITIONAL
BRAINWASHING

The umpteen smokers who quit for ten years then started again or are still moping about how they miss them. Ex-smokers who tell you how great they feel and who next time you see them are puffing away again. Smokers who are clearly killing themselves yet still smoke. And the misery of your own failed attempts when using willpower.

THE WILLPOWER METHOD

Something triggers an attempt to quit. The smoker forces himself into a self-imposed tantrum, like a child being deprived of candy, hoping that if he has the willpower to resist the temptation long enough, one day he will wake up with the feeling

EUREKA! I'M FREE!!!

Why He Never Achieves It

After a few days the congestion goes, you have more money, no longer despise yourself, and have that wonderful holier-than-thou feeling of no longer being a slave. All the reasons that made you decide to quit are rapidly disappearing. Meanwhile, the "Little Monster" hasn't had his fix—your brain is saying:

"I WANT A CIGARETTE!"

THE CONFUSION

For some mysterious reason you still want a cigarette but aren't allowed to have one. You start to feel deprived and miserable. This is one of the occasions your brain has been programmed to light a cigarette, so you feel even more miserable. Soon your whole life is dominated by the misery of not being allowed to smoke.

Eventually Your Willpower Runs Out

You get fed up with always feeling miserable. You start searching for reasons to have just one cigarette, and eventually you find one. The longer you have abstained, the weirder that first cigarette tastes. The longer you have suffered the misery of feeling deprived, the greater the illusion of pleasure. You are soon back to where you started.

ABSENCE MAKES THE HEART GROW FONDER

If you believe there is some genuine pleasure in smoking, why should that belief ever go? The "Little Monster" is identical to normal hunger and normal stress. So, long after the "Little Monster" has died, during times of normal hunger or stress, the ex-smoker's brain is still fooled into believing that a cigarette will help.

IT'S CONFLICT,
NOT LACK OF WILLPOWER

At our clinics we ask smokers who think they are weak-willed: "If you ran out late at night, how far would you walk for a pack of cigarettes?"

A smoker would swim the English Channel for a pack. A strong-willed child will keep his tantrum going forever. It takes a strong-willed person to block his mind to the terrible health risks and continue to smoke.

I Knew That
I Was Strong-Willed

I couldn't understand why no one and nothing else in my life controlled me, yet I was completely dominated by something I loathed. Or why my friends could smoke ten cigarettes a day and I had to chain-smoke. It never occurred to me that they couldn't afford to chain-smoke, or that their lungs couldn't cope with the poison.

NATIONAL NO-SMOKING DAY

According to the media, that's the day every smoker attempts to quit. In reality, it's the day every smoker smokes twice as many and twice as blatantly, because smokers don't like being told what to do by people who don't understand. It takes a strong-willed person to resist the massive antisocial pressures that smokers are subjected to nowadays.

CHECK OUT YOUR SMOKING FRIENDS

The main illusion about smoking is that it relieves stress. It is physical and mentally dominant people who tend to take up highly responsible professions. You'll find that your acquaintances who are still heavy smokers are strong-willed in other ways. We are about to remove this conflict of wills.

How Does
"EASYWAY" Work?

By simply removing the confusion and misconceptions that make it difficult to quit. Smokers try to "give up" smoking. This implies a genuine sacrifice. For the reasons I have already explained, there is absolutely nothing to give up.

The two monsters create the illusion of pleasure or crutch. The reality is the complete opposite.

THE ADVANTAGES OF BEING A SMOKER

There aren't any. I don't mean the disadvantages outweigh them. I mean there is no pleasure or crutch whatsoever. On the contrary, smoking destroys your nerves and confidence and creates boredom, restlessness, and dissatisfaction. Far from being your friend, it would be difficult to imagine a worse enemy.

It's Fear That Keeps Us Smoking

A subtlety of the nicotine trap is to keep its victims trapped for life.

You might feel that I'm taking away and giving nothing back. You might be tempted to stop reading or to abandon your attempt. Please don't fall for the trap. Like me, ex-smokers who used my method found it to be the most rewarding experience of their lives.

SNUFF-TAKING

Sniffing dried tobacco is a form of nicotine addiction. Like smoking, it was regarded as a habit. Addicts used similar gimmicks, such as silver snuff-boxes, to disguise the filth. Do heroin addicts enjoy injections? Do cocaine sniffers enjoy sniffing for sniffing's sake? Or are these just the rather disgusting methods we use to administer the drug?

I Enjoy the Ritual

Smokers believe that there is an actual pleasure in smoking, and that the health risks and expense are merely hazards that interfere with that pleasure. If that were true, smokers would enjoy herbal cigarettes. They never do. Smoking is merely a more dangerous and disgusting form of nicotine addiction.

A Moment To Reflect

If you are not yet convinced that there is nothing to give up and that the pleasure or crutch from smoking is merely an ingenious confidence trick, it is essential that you stop reading at this stage, go back to the beginning, and start again. Remember, I have nothing but good news for you, provided you follow my instructions.

WHAT ARE YOU
TRYING TO ACHIEVE?

Never to smoke again? No. This is what smokers who use willpower do. They go through the rest of their lives hoping they'll never smoke again. Which means they don't achieve their object until they die. This means they never know whether or not they succeeded.

WHEN DO YOU BECOME A NON-SMOKER?

It is important that you reflect on this question. Typical answers are:

When I stop thinking about smoking.

How do you stop thinking about it?

When I can enjoy a meal or answer the phone, etc., without craving a cigarette.

How long will that be?

When I've quit for a year.

Why wait a year? Why not longer?

It's all so vague and indecisive.

WHAT ARE YOU TRYING TO ACHIEVE!

The real difference between a smoker and a non-smoker is not that the latter doesn't smoke but that he has no desire to smoke. If you have no desire to smoke, there is no temptation to smoke and therefore no need for willpower to resist the temptation.

A FRAME OF MIND

What you are trying to achieve is a frame of mind, so that when you extinguish the final cigarette, for the next few days and for the rest of your life, whenever you think about smoking, instead of thinking, "I'd love a cigarette" or "When will I be free?", you say to yourself:

> "EUREKA! I'M ALREADY FREE!
> I'M ALREADY A NON-SMOKER!"

HOW WILL YOU KNOW
THAT YOU ARE FREE?

By clearing up all the doubts and confusion before you extinguish the final cigarette. By realizing that there is no such thing as a special or occasional cigarette, only a lifetime's chain of misery. By realizing that you are giving up absolutely nothing. On the contrary, you are receiving marvelous positive gains.

THOSE MARVELOUS POSITIVE GAINS

I knew I was literally burning my hard-earned money and risking terrible diseases. The chain reaction was like a time bomb ticking away inside my body, never knowing the length of the fuse, hoping I would quit before it went off. It's great to be free of the fear and self-loathing, but there were even greater, unexpected gains.

THE LETHARGY

I knew the coughing and congestion were due to smoking, but I thought the lack of energy was due to old age. I struggled to get up in the morning, and fell asleep each evening watching TV. It's great to wake up full of energy and feeling that you've had a good night's rest, actually wanting to exercise and feeling like a young boy again.

The Fear

As a youth, I enjoyed physicals, believing I was indestructible. As a smoker, I hated them. I even hated visiting other people in hospitals. The mere thought of chest x-rays would create panic. I was convinced that cigarettes gave me courage. It's so great to feel strong again, able to enjoy the good times and being fully equipped to cope with the bad.

THE SLAVERY

So intent was I on resisting all the attempts of the do-gooders who were trying to inform me of what I already knew—SMOKERS ARE FOOLS—it never occurred to me that I spent half my life feeling miserable because I wasn't allowed to smoke and the other half miserable because I did.

IT'S SO LOVELY BEING FREE!

A SOCIABLE PASTIME?

It's about as sociable as farting in an elevator! In the old days you could visit a strange office or a friend's house and ask, "Do you mind if I smoke?" It was really a polite way of asking for an ashtray. Ask for an ashtray nowadays and people look at you as if you are requesting some relic of the distant past. Smokers regard themselves as social pariahs.

THE SINISTER BLACK SHADOW

All our lives the fear of quitting makes us block our minds to the bad effects of smoking. It's like an ever-increasing black shadow forming in our subconscious. Strong people hate being controlled by something they loathe. The greatest gain is to be free of this dark cloud and self-loathing and to genuinely pity rather than envy smokers.

THE FIRST POWERFUL INFLUENCE

Before I started smoking, life was exciting. I could enjoy the highs and handle the stresses. When I finally discovered the "EASYWAY" to quit, it was like waking from a nightmare, escaping from a black-and-white world of fear and depression into a sunshine world of health, confidence, and freedom. I still can't get over the euphoria.

THE SECOND POWERFUL INFLUENCE

All creatures on this planet instinctively know the difference between food and poison. Even before that first experimental cigarette, we know that there is something evil and unnatural about breathing lethal fumes into our lungs. To have to do it all day, every day, because of the influence of a subtle, sinister drug, is not only evil but unthinkable.

THE CORRECT DECISION

Some decisions are difficult to make. How can you be certain that a particular car or TV is the best value for you? There is one decision in your life, however, that is easy to make: whether to spend the rest of your life as a smoker or a non-smoker. Smoking provides no advantages whatsoever and horrendous disadvantages.

IF YOU HESITATE

It's not because you are too stupid to see the obvious—you don't even need me to tell you the correct decision—it's because of FEAR! The greatest gain is to be free of that fear, which is caused by the drug. You never decided to become a smoker, but fell into an ingenious trap that is designed to enslave you for life.

THE INGENUITY OF THE TRAP

We are fooled into believing that we smoke because of some genuine pleasure or crutch. Therefore, we don't decide to quit until we have stress in our lives, such as a money shortage or bad health. But these are exactly the times we most need our little *"friend."* If we quit, the reasons why we quit soon disappear, so we start smoking again.

WHY THE TIME WILL NEVER BE RIGHT

Because the times you most need to quit are the times you most need your little *"friend."* Because there will always be some occasion coming up shortly in your life, be it social or stressful, that will enable you to put off the evil day. That's part of the ingenuity of the trap. Be aware of it! Don't fall for it!

SOME SMOKERS JUST DRIFT OUT OF IT

Rather like they drifted into it. I waited thirty-three years, hoping that would happen to me. Believe me, it will no more happen than you would drift out of a bear trap. You will only escape if you make a positive effort to do so, and the first step is to make the decision to make that attempt. I want you to do that now.

It Takes Courage

And I want you to have the courage to make that decision now. I'm not asking you to smoke your final cigarette now—I'll advise you when to do that—but merely to make the decision that you'll go for it. If you have the courage to do that and follow my instructions to the letter, you will not only find it easy but enjoyable.

A FEELING OF DOOM AND GLOOM

If you have such a feeling, dismiss it now. You are about to achieve something marvelous, something that every smoker on the planet would love to achieve: TO BE FREE! It's a no-lose proposition. If you don't succeed, you are no worse off. But let's not even think of failure. After all, it was you Americans who taught the rest of the world not just to reach for the moon, but to actually land on it! Start right now with a feeling of excitement, challenge, and elation.

How Do I Cope With the Withdrawal?

The actual physical withdrawal from nicotine is no worse when you quit than throughout your smoking life. Although nicotine is the world's most powerful drug in the speed with which it hooks you, the good news is that you are never badly hooked. Smokers experience physical withdrawal from nicotine their whole smoking lives. If a smoker sleeps for six hours a night, when he wakes he is 97% nicotine-free. He has been going through withdrawal the entire night, but it's so mild that it doesn't even wake him up!

SO WHY DO SMOKERS GET SO IRRITABLE?

For exactly the same reason they get into a panic when they run out of cigarettes. Smokers don't wake up in a panic, even though they've gone eight hours without nicotine. Most smokers nowadays will leave the bedroom or eat breakfast before they light their first cigarette. Others will wait till they arrive at work.

THAT PANICKED FEELING

It can start even before you run out. You're at a party and ration your cigarettes, saving one for bedtime and one for the morning. Some joker says: "Do you mind if I have one of yours?" As you meekly hand it over, you're thinking: *Mind? Of course I mind! I'd rather give you a pint of blood or even donate a kidney!*

ADDICTION IS MENTAL, NOT PHYSICAL

The almost imperceptible physical discomfort created by the "Little Monster" acts as a catalyst that triggers the "Big Monster." It's the "Big Monster" that creates the fear and panic—the belief that we cannot enjoy or cope with life without nicotine. Fortunately, we can remove the illusion, fear, and panic, prior to the final cigarette.

BE AWARE OF THE "LITTLE MONSTER"

For a few days after quitting, the "Little Monster" will live on. You might be aware of a feeling of insecurity or merely think: *"I want a cigarette."* This is when ex-smokers get confused and miserable because they can't have one. They believe they are being deprived of a genuine pleasure or crutch.

BE PREPARED FOR
THAT FEELING

But don't worry about it. Recognize it for what it is. Say to yourself, *"It's what smokers feel throughout their smoking lives and what keeps them miserable, poor, lethargic, unhealthy slaves!"*

Rejoice in the fact that you have already escaped from the prison. Revel in the death throes of the "Little Monster"!

ESCAPED OR TRYING TO ESCAPE?

You become a non-smoker the moment you extinguish your final cigarette. *But how do you know it is your final cigarette?* Simply by removing all doubt and uncertainty first. If you have doubts, you are merely hoping not to smoke again. How will you ever know? You'll be waiting for nothing to happen, and like so many ex-smokers, will do so the rest of your life.

But How Can You Ever Be Certain?

Would you take up a pastime that gave you no pleasure or advantages whatsoever, that cost you a fortune, shortened your life, and made you feel nervous, lethargic, unclean, stupid, and miserable? The biggest idiot on earth wouldn't! Having made what you know to be the correct decision, never punish yourself by ever doubting it!

Oh, I'd Love a Cigarette!

How often do you hear ex-smokers, whether they have quit for a few hours, days, or even years, make similar statements? It is these whining stoppers who make existing smokers frightened to even make the attempt—they perpetuate the belief that once a smoker always a smoker, that once addicted you can never be completely free!

IT'S ABSOLUTE NONSENSE!!!

How Stupid Can You Get?

Why do otherwise intelligent people decide to quit, then spend the rest of their lives bemoaning the fact that they can't smoke the occasional cigarette? It's because they doubt their decision, they believe that they have made a genuine sacrifice, that they actually received some genuine pleasure or crutch from smoking.

In Reality, It's Even More Stupid!

What they are moping for never actually existed. For example, the favorite cigarettes, such as the one after a meal. Can you ever actually remember thinking: *"This really tastes marvelous"*?

Isn't it true that it's not so much that we enjoy smoking cigarettes, but that we assume we do, because we are miserable without them?

REMEMBER THOSE STRESSFUL SITUATIONS

When your car broke down in the pouring rain in the middle of nowhere, and you were soaking wet and covered in grease, can you remember lighting up and thinking: *"I'm late for the most important appointment of my life. But who cares? I've got this gorgeous pack of cigarettes!"*?

Did they make you happy and cheerful?

I Can't Answer the Phone Without One

A common plea of the many powerful business executives who attend our clinics. What's so stressful about the phone? It won't blow up or bite you. It's that little itch that's causing the stress. That's also why smokers find it difficult to concentrate without first removing the distraction. Non-smokers don't seem to suffer from the problem.

BUT IT DEFINITELY RELIEVES BOREDOM

Does it? Boredom is a frame of mind. When you smoke a cigarette, do you sit there thinking: *"Oh, how mind-absorbing and fascinating this is"*? Can you think of anything more boring than chain-smoking cigarette after cigarette, day in, day out, for thirty-three years, as I once did? We smoke when bored, because there is nothing to distract us from the itch.

NEVER DOUBT YOUR DECISION

It's the uncertainty that makes it difficult to quit. Having made what you know to be the correct decision, never punish yourself by questioning that decision. If you see one cigarette as a pleasure or crutch, you'll see a million cigarettes that way. By craving one, you'll be miserable because you can't have it, and even more miserable if you do!

THE GREATEST MISTAKE

Smokers make when they try to quit is to try not to think about smoking. This merely creates a phobia. Remember that something marvelous is happening. It's what you are thinking that's important. If it's: *"I can't have one"* or *"when will I be free?"* you'll be doubting your decision. Instead always think:

YIPPEE! I'M A NON-SMOKER!!!

"THE MOMENT OF REVELATION"

If you follow the instructions, after just a few days you'll have a moment—it might be in a social or stressful situation, one of those times that you thought you could never enjoy or handle without a cigarette—when not only did you enjoy or handle it, but you never even thought about smoking. That's when you know you are free!

Don't Wait For It To Happen

If you try to force "The Moment of Revelation," it will be like worrying about not being able to sleep— you'll merely ensure it won't happen. You become a non-smoker the moment you cut off the supply of nicotine. Just get on with your life. Accept that you'll have good days and bad, just as smokers do.

Don't Change
Your Lifestyle

Just because you've quit smoking: things such as avoiding your smoking friends. If you do, you'll be miserable. Remember you aren't giving up living. You aren't giving up anything. On the contrary, as your energy level and confidence improve, you'll find both your capacity to enjoy life and to handle stress will increase.

It All Happens So Slowly

Another ingenuity of the nicotine trap is that our slide down into the pit is so gradual that we aren't even aware of the increasing debilitation of our physical and mental health. The problem is that when we quit, the recovery is also gradual, and if we are using the willpower method and feeling miserable and deprived, we tend to be blind to the immense gains.

"It Takes Seven Years to Clear The Gunk"

Or, "Every cigarette you smoke takes five minutes off your life." Such statements are true, but only if you contract one of the killer diseases. If you quit now, your health can recover up to 99%, as if you'd never been a smoker, and the bulk of the gunk goes away during the first few days and weeks.

USE YOUR IMAGINATION

If it were possible to project any smoker three weeks ahead to give him a direct comparison of how he would feel as a non-smoker, not just physically but in terms of confidence, he would have no hesitation in quitting cheerfully and immediately. I can't do that, but you can:

JUST USE YOUR IMAGINATION!

Time Is on Your Side

Provided that you've first removed the brainwashing, once you've cut off the supply of nicotine, nothing can prevent you from being free. You will already be a non-smoker, and it is essential that you think of yourself as one immediately. If you wait for it to happen, it will be like sowing seeds, then watching the ground until they grow.

EXPECT SOME DISORIENTATION

Even changes for the better, like a new job, house, or car, involve a period of adjustment. If you do feel somewhat strange at first, that will soon go, provided that you don't start worrying about it. Remember, any slight aggravation you might suffer is not because you've quit but because you started in the first place. Non-smokers don't suffer from withdrawal.

I KEEP FORGETTING
I'VE QUIT

Don't worry! It's quite normal and a good sign. It means that already your mind isn't completely obsessed. But these are the times when those who've stopped through willpower start to doubt and mope. Train yourself to reverse the moment immediately. Remind yourself how lucky you are to be free, or just think: YIPPEE! I'M A NON-SMOKER! That way those moments become pleasurable.

I Can't Get Up Without a Cigarette

When you extinguish that final cigarette, look forward to being free the rest of the day. Lie in bed, reflecting that you have already achieved the most difficult part—making the start and anticipating the exciting challenge of proving you can not only survive but actually enjoy a whole day, from dawn to dusk, FREE!!!

It Happens on Social Occasions

You're chatting away, oblivious. The cigarettes are handed around. You find yourself subconsciously taking one. Your friend smirks, "I thought you'd given them up!" You feel stupid. Don't just stand there. Instead say, "I'd quite forgotten." (Which is all that happened.) "I can't tell you how lovely it is to be free. You should try it!" The situation is reversed.

NEVER ENVY SMOKERS

There is a constant battle between smokers and ex-smokers. As more and more smokers leave the sinking ship, those left on it feel more stupid, insecure, and isolated. This fear can cause even people who love you to try to get you hooked again. Never forget that the ex-smoker holds all the aces, and the smoker doesn't even have a pair of twos!

ATTEND SOCIAL FUNCTIONS IMMEDIATELY

Even if you are the only non-smoker present (usually the reverse now), always be aware that every one of those smokers would love to be like you. They will expect you to be miserable. When they see you happy and cheerful, they'll think you are a Superman or Superwoman.

The important point is:

YOU'LL FEEL LIKE ONE!
ENJOY YOUR ESCAPE!

WHEN WILL THE CRAVING GO?

The "Little Monster" causes the physical itch to your body. But it is only your brain that is capable of craving a cigarette. For a few days the "Little Monster" might continue to trigger the thought: "I want a cigarette." Your brain has the choice of craving one or recognizing the feeling for what it is and thinking:

"YIPPEE! I'M A NON-SMOKER!!!"

WHEN A FRIEND OR RELATIVE DIES

You have to go through a period of mourning. Eventually, time partially heals the wound and life goes on. It's the same with people who stop smoking through willpower. If they can suffer the misery long enough, life goes on. But they still believe they've given up a genuine pleasure or crutch. Come a trauma in their lives, smoke one cigarette, and they're back in the trap!

WHEN AN ENEMY DIES

You don't have to go through a mourning process. You can rejoice immediately and for the rest of your life. The cigarette was never a friend. It was the worst disease you'll ever suffer from. You have it in your control. You have the choice of spending the next few days moping for an illusion or rejoicing:

"YIPPEE! I'M A NON-SMOKER!!!"

I NEED A SUBSTITUTE

I presume that you are searching for some elixir that will have contradictory effects like relieving boredom and helping concentration, relieving stress and improving relaxation, and which at the same time won't destroy your health and wealth. If you ever find it, please let me know. By the way, do you search for Aladdin's lamp?

Do Not Use Substitutes

By even searching for one, you are confirming that you are making a sacrifice: "There is a void in my life. I need something to take its place." When you get rid of a bout of the flu, do you search for a substitute disease? Nicotine created the void. You didn't need to smoke before you became hooked. Substitutes merely prolong the feeling of a void.

WILL I PUT ON WEIGHT?

Only if you substitute candy or gum, or start picking between meals. If you do, not only will you get fat and miserable, but you won't even satisfy the empty feeling and will prolong your search for illusory rewards. If you put on a couple of pounds due to a better appetite at main meals, don't worry. When you've kicked smoking, you can control anything, and will soon be able to lose them.

WILL NICOTINE GUM OR PATCHES HELP?

NO! In theory, while you are breaking the habit, they ease the terrible physical withdrawal pains, and when you've broken the habit, you wean yourself off the nicotine substitute. In fact, the physical withdrawal is almost imperceptible, and it's not habit but addiction. They keep the "Little Monster" alive and the "Big Monster" craving!

Enjoy Having a Non-Smoke

If you cannot visualize certain activities without smoking, break the association from the start. Have your drink, do your crossword puzzle, whatever. Enjoy being a non-smoker. Enjoy not only removing the gunk from your body but also proving that you can enjoy life without smoking. It's only smokers who can't enjoy life without nicotine.

I'll Have To Give Up Golf

In fact, you will not have to give up anything. I couldn't visualize even wanting to play golf without smoking. In fact, I couldn't visualize life without cigarettes. Now I can't visualize that I was once a nicotine slave. Soon, you'll find it difficult to understand why you ever felt the need to smoke, and wonder why you can't make other smokers appreciate just how nice it is to be free!

OBSERVE CASUAL SMOKERS AT PARTIES

They almost chain-smoke! Notice how agitated they are when not smoking. Watch the obvious relief when they light up. Observe how quickly the cigarette burns and watch the increasing agitation when the nicotine leaves. Remember, the next day they have to continue the chain, ad infinitum, for life!

Observe Smokers Generally

Watch young girls smoking in the street, drivers in a traffic jam, office workers outside a non-smoking office, vacationers whose flight has been delayed, or lone smokers at a social function. Notice they don't even seem to be aware that they are smoking, or, if they are, how uncomfortable they look, and how even more miserable they are, when not allowed to smoke.

TIMING

The natural tendency is to pick a period when you feel you least need a cigarette. Like practically every other aspect about smoking, the correct course is the complete opposite. Start at a time you consider to be the most difficult, prove straight away that you can enjoy the social occasion or handle the stress, and the rest is easy.

A DEGENERATIVE DISEASE

With a disease that gets worse and worse, it doesn't take a Sherlock Holmes to deduce that the quicker you get rid of it the better. If you had Alzheimer's or Parkinson's disease and there were a simple cure, would you delay a single day? Smoking is the Number One killer disease in society. Fortunately, there is a simple cure:

DO IT NOW!

THE FINAL PREPARATION

You should now be like a dog straining at the leash to smoke that final cigarette. If not, there can only be two reasons: that you do not believe that smoking conveys no advantages whatsoever—if so, read back from the beginning—or that you believe but still have a feeling of doom and gloom. In which case, stop being stupid and trust me.

THE FINAL CIGARETTE

I want you to smoke it, not with a feeling of doom and gloom but with a feeling of elation. Did you decide to fall into the trap? Just think how great the Count of Monte Cristo felt when he finally escaped from that prison. Don't extinguish that final cigarette thinking: *"I must never smoke again."* Rather:

> *"ISN'T IT MARVELOUS —*
> *I DON'T EVER NEED TO!"*

NEVER ENVY SMOKERS

You are not being deprived. If you see someone smoking, no matter what the occasion, be aware that they are not smoking because they choose to. They are being deprived of their money, health, energy, relaxation, self-respect, and freedom. All that, to achieve what? Nothing! Just trying to feel like a non-smoker. Smokers are drug addicts, and like all drug addiction — it'll just get worse and worse.

HELP THEM!

ALLEN CARR IN THE USA

For more information on Allen Carr's Easyway Clinics and services in the USA contact:

TOLL FREE   1-866-NO-NIC-99
                    1-866-666-4299

e-mail: reservations@allencarrusa.com
website: www.allencarr.com

ALLEN CARR'S WORLDWIDE HEAD OFFICE

Allen Carr's Easyway International Ltd
1c Amity Grove, London SW20 OLQ ENGLAND
+44 (0)20 8944 7761

e-mail: postmaster@allencarr.demon.co.uk

For details of Allen Carr's worldwide network of clinics visit www.allencarr.com

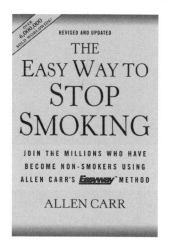